Key Stage 2

Level 3

Spelling Made Easy

Teacher's Textbook
(Revised)

Best selling Multi-Sensory Structured Phonics

by Violet Brand

Age Group 10 - 11 Years

Introduction

Violet Brand's highly successful 'Spelling Made Easy' series originated in her diagnostic work with young adults with reading difficulties between 1975 and 1980. Multi-sensory phonic-based reading and spelling methods were unfashionable at the time so she created her own teaching material. This was published in 1984 and became widely used, in particular for one-to-one tuition.

Violet always maintained that if a pupil could spell they could read.

The Revised 'Spelling Made Easy' Text Books (publ 2012) are faithful to the original structure and sequence but the range has been updated to include:

- Expanded initial word lists to encompass early introduction of the synthetic phonics sequence
- Synthetic phonics sequence highlighted in Red Introductory Book
- Additional material included in Red Introductory Level and Green Level 1 books
- New 'pupil friendly' typeface
- Texts modernised and updated as required with completely new text for Purple Book Level 3

The highly important original features of the series are still present including:

- The clearly defined incremental sequence of sounds including phonemes and blends
- Word lists for each sound to be taught word by word in a 'listen, say and write' sequence. Violet Brand's original suggested teaching method, using the 'a' sound for instance, was:

    (a) Write the sound in red on a board – saying it

    (b) Show card with the family of words written in 'blackboard' size

    (c) Cover all words but 'cat' – children read it

    (d) Gradually uncover all words until full list is seen and read

    (e) Draw attention of children to common sound/symbol in all of the words

    (f) Pupils write the words as teacher dictates them

    (g) Encourage all pupils to quietly say the sounds as they write them

- A dictation accompanies each new word list for pupils to write out and then identify words with the featured sounds
- 'High frequency' words are introduced early
- 'Teaching points' focus on possible areas of difficulty with practical suggestions to work on these.

BrandBooks 2012

Contents

Sound	Page	Sound	Page
a-e	1	Soft g	17
i-e	2	ar	18
o-e	3	ous	19
u-e	4	ary/able	20
Double consonant/short vowel 1	5	le	21
ur	6	er	22
tion	7	y (ĭ)	23
Soft c	8	sion	24
Double consonant/short vowel 2	9	ie/ei	25
ful	10	ent/ence	26
ch (k)	11	al ending	27
ly	12	y (i)	28
or	13	ea (ē)	29
Silent letter 1	14	our	30
Silent letter 2	15	ance/ant	31
ough/eigh	16	Apostrophe	32

Additional and ancillary material for the sounds listed above is available in Spelling Made Easy 'Fun with Phonics' Level 3 Worksheets (Page references in brackets)

a-e, i-e, o-e, u-e — Fun with Phonics pp 2-5
Various double consonants 1, ur, tion — Fun with Phonics pp 6-9
Various, soft c, Double consonants 2, ful — Fun with Phonics pp 10-13
ch (k), ly, or — Fun with Phonics pp 14-17
Silent letters 1 and 2, ough/eigh — Fun with Phonics pp 18-21
Soft g, ar, ous, ary/able — Fun with Phonics pp 22-25
le, er, y (ĭ) — Fun with Phonics pp 26-29
sion, ie/ei, ent/ence — Fun with Phonics pp 30-33
al, y (i), ea (ē) — Fun with Phonics pp 34-37
our, ance/ant — Fun with Phonics pp 38-41

Spelling Made Easy Level 3 A4 Text Book (Revised)
by Violet Brand
First published in the United Kingdom in 2012

© Copyright assigned to BrandBooks (a division of G & M Brand Publications Ltd) and Violet Brand who asserts her moral rights as the author.

ISBN 978-1-904421-23-8 All rights reserved. www.spellingmadeeasy.co.uk

The copyright of all materials in the 'Spelling Made Easy' series remains the property of the publisher and the author. No part of this book may be reproduced or translated in any form or by any means, electronic or mechanical, including recording or by an information storage or retrieval system without permission in writing from the publisher.

"The multi-sensory methods of teaching spelling seem to have been overlooked in recent main-stream education. Too much emphasis has been placed on learning to spell through visual methods. The ears and the mouth have been forgotten and the power of the hand ignored.

If a child, or an adult, hears a sequence of sounds, sees them visually represented, feels the sequence in their mouth and reproduces the symbols with their hand, their awareness of the basis of written language is awakened. They feel that they can control it - and what they control they can use. No one sense is left to flounder and the fear of the printed word which so often besets adult illiterates and failing teenagers is removed"

(Violet Brand MBE Introduction to 1984 editions)

a–e

  chocol**a**t**e**   b**a**s**e**
  desp<u>er</u>**a**t**e**   b**a**s**e**d
a<u>cc</u>o<u>mm</u>od**a**t**e**   persu**a**d**e**
  evap<u>or</u>**a**t**e**   W**a**l**e**s
  evap<u>or</u>**a**t**e**d
  exa<u>gg</u>er**a**t**e**   **a**g**e**
             ag**e**s
  fortun**a**t**e**   mess**a**g**e**
  fortun**a**t**e**ly   dam**a**g**e**
  immedi**a**t**e**ly   ch**a**ng**e**
  dilapid**a**t**e**d   str**a**ng**e**
  sep<u>ar</u>**a**t**e**
  s**a**f**e**ly
  s**a**f**e**ty

Dictate the Sam Story

 Sam is on his way home from work on his dilapidated old bike. He is desperate for a bar of chocolate. Since the age of nine, Sam has loved chocolate. It is not possible to exaggerate how much he loves it. Sam goes into a little shop to get some, but he does not have any change in his pocket. He has to persuade the shop owner to let him take a bar of chocolate and bring the money later. Fortunately the shop owner is in a good mood and is willing to help, but he does think Sam is a little strange.

Teaching Points

(a) Identify with the pupils the common 'a-e' element in each word.
(b) Draw attention to the tricky parts underlined.
(c) Discuss word meanings, in particular, 'dilapidated' and 'exaggerate'.
(d) Talk about favourite foods in general.
(e) Discuss how small shops work and how they make money by buying things at cost price, and then increase the price to make a profit.
(f) Discuss the pros and cons of small independent shops versus large supermarket chains.
(g) Ask the pupils to write a short piece, no more than 50 words, on their favourite food.

i–e

arrive	admire
arrived	acquire
decide	tire
decided	tired
advertise	retire
advertisement	require
recognise	umpire
	Ireland
definite	
definitely	likely
indefinitely	tie
excite	tied
excitement	ninety
excitedly	nineteen
quite	

Dictate the Sam Story

Sam is excited because he is going to watch a rugby match between Wales and Ireland. Sam admires the rugby players as they can run around for so long without getting tired. He decides to arrive early so he can find a good place to sit. At half-time, Sam has an ice-cream. He thinks it is likely that Wales will win, but in the end it is a tie, with nineteen points to each team. As the players retire to the changing rooms, Sam thinks he will definitely come again as he has had such a great time.

Teaching Points

(a) Identify common elements. Draw particular attention to the 'ire' words and the position of 'e' in 'definitely' and 'nineteen'.
(b) Discuss word meanings, particularly, 'retire' and 'tie'.
(c) Discuss favourite sports, both to watch and to play.
(d) Discuss the importance of fitness in everyday life.
(e) Discuss the importance of playing in a team and what we can learn from both winning and losing games.
(f) Let the pupils design a poster for an upcoming sports match, whether in school or in professional sports.

o–e

chose
clothes
compose
disclose
pose

explode
episode
erode
lonely
loneliness

hopeless
slope
scone
zone
quote

probe
whole
joe
hoe
oboe
tomatoes
potatoes

hotel
motel

Dictate the Sam Story

Sam is staying in a hotel. He is eating a plate of chicken and potatoes when the police arrive to probe a report of a missing man. They tell Sam the stranger has disappeared on the mountain slopes. He was wearing old clothes and had only a couple of scones and his trombone with him. Sam thinks the man was trying to compose music for his trombone, but two other guests disclose that they heard something explode on the slopes. The police are still in the zone, looking for the man with their dogs. Sam hopes they find the lonely man. He has been put off his potatoes.

Teaching Points
(a) Discuss word meanings.
(b) Draw attention to the position of 'e' in lonely, loneliness and hopeless.
(c) Point out tomato and potato, but tomatoes and potatoes.
(d) Ask the pupils whether they have ever stayed in a hotel and what they liked and disliked about it.
(e) Talk about the trombone. Show the pupils pictures and play a recording of one.
(f) Following dictation, ask the pupils to write the next episode of this story, in no more than 100 words.

u–e

```
       argue                              sure
    continue                            unsure
    continued                           assure
         due                          pressure
       pursue
        queue                          capture
                                     departure
       acute                           failure
     dispute                            figure
  substitute                        literature
     include                       temperature
     exclude
      consume
       rebuke

         use
      accuse
      disuse
      disused
```

Dictate the Sam Story

Sam's train is due for departure at 11.07 and he is standing in a queue, waiting to purchase a ticket. Then a woman's voice comes over the loudspeaker to say that due to a signal failure there will be a delay. The woman is unsure how long the delay will last, but she wishes to assure passengers that they are doing all they can to find a substitute train. The temperature is high and people begin to argue. Sam uses the extra time to consume a huge bag of chicken and chips so by the time the new train is found, he is feeling quite ill.

Teaching Points

(a) Look at the various sections within this family – 'ue' ending, 'use', 'sure' and 'ure'.
(b) Discuss meanings, particularly 'substitute' and 'consume'.
(c) Discuss temperatures – body and weather. Show thermometers and maps, and discuss how temperature can differ around the world, and the effect this can have on lifestyle and health.
(d) Talk about train journeys and briefly explain how the railways began, showing pictures of steam trains and modern day trains.
(e) After dictation, ask the pupils to write a description of a train journey they have been on in no more than 100 words.

Double consonant/short vowel 1

a **dd** r e s s
a **tt** i c
b e g i **nn** i n g
b u **tt** e r f l y
d a **gg** e r
d i **nn** e r

d i s a **pp** e a r
d i s a **pp** o i n t
d i s a **pp** o i n t e d
e m b a **rr** a **ss**
f i **tt** e d
f i **ll** e d

f o **gg** y
h a **pp** e n
h i **dd** e n
j e w e **ll** e r y
m a **mm** <u>a</u> l
n a **r** r <u>a</u> t i v e

r e c o **mm** e n d
s l i **pp** e d
v a **ll** e y
w i **nn** i n g

Dictate the Sam Story

Sam wants to take his wife Sue out for dinner so he asks Gus to recommend somewhere nice. Sam has also got Sue some jewellery which he will hide in her pudding. Sam wants Sue to have a great time. Gus gives Sam the address. It is in a valley next to a river, but it is foggy and Sam gets lost on the way and they end up in a different place. Sam is embarrassed and Sue is disappointed. Sam wishes he could go back to the beginning and start again, but it is too late. He decides to give Sue the jewellery in the car. She loves her gift, and smiles at Sam. "These things happen," she says.

"Yes, but why do they always happen to me?" asks Sam.

Teaching Points
(a) Remind that a double consonant keeps the vowel short. Show the pupils the difference between dinner and dining room.
(b) Discuss the prefix 'dis' and its negative effect.
(c) Discuss word meanings, such as 'embarrass' and 'recommend'.
(d) Discuss rivers and valleys. Talk briefly about how valleys are made, and show pictures.
(e) Ask the pupils to name different sorts of jewellery.
(f) After dictation, if there's time, ask the pupils to draw a design for a piece of jewellery and colour it in.

ur

absurd
burglar
burgle
further
gurgle

hurdle
hurl
hurtle
murder
murmur

occur
occurred
purchase
pursue
purpose

suburb
surge
surgeon
surprise

survey
survive
turnstile
urgent

Dictate the Sam Story

Sue hides the jewellery Sam purchased for her as a surprise gift. She puts it in a safe she purchased for the purpose of keeping all her jewellery safe from burglars. Sam and Sue live in a quiet suburb, and there is a turnstile at the end of their street, so burglars hardly ever try to burgle houses in the area. In a survey, people living in Sam's suburb said they felt happy walking home at night and there was very little crime. Sam says he would pursue a burglar if he had to, or make an urgent call to the police.

Teaching Points

(a) After discussing the common 'ur' element in these words, draw attention to the endings of burglar, further, murder and murmur. 'Further' and 'murder' are the most predictable, as 'er' usually makes that sound at the end of the word.
(b) Look at the 'ey' ending of survey and point out the 'e' in surgeon – to soften the 'g'.
(c) Discuss suburbs – in relation to cities.
(d) Discuss ways in which can keep our belongings safe.
(e) Discuss why it is wrong to steal from other people and shops.
(f) After the dictation, ask the pupils to draw a picture of Sam pursuing a burglar down the street, and getting stuck in the turnstile.

tion

st**ation**	ac**tion**
alter**ation**	condi**tion**
accomm<u>o</u>d**ation**	corr<u>e</u>c**tion**
convers**ation**	descrip**tion**
educ**ation**	direc**tion**
examin**ation**	e<u>x</u>cep**tion**
invit**ation**	frac**tion**
resp<u>i</u>r**ation**	inte<u>rr</u>up**tion**
sep<u>ar</u>**ation**	rep<u>e</u>ti**tion**
situ**ation**	produc**tion**
prep<u>ar</u>**ation**	
punctu**ation**	atten**tion**
	inven**tion**
	men**tion**
	objec**tion**

Dictate the Sam Story

   Sam has gone back into education to get better qualifications. He has an examination in one week and has asked Sue to help him, so she sets him some questions. It is a maths examination and Sam is no good at fractions. Sue makes lots of corrections. She has a conversation with Sam and tells him he must take action and give more attention to his preparation or he may fail the test. Sam decides not to mention the spelling examination he must also take because his punctuation is as bad as his fractions. He goes to meet Gus to discuss the situation.

Teaching Points

(a) Point out that all the words in column one end in 'ation'.
(b) Discuss the tricky parts underlined.
(c) Discuss why it is so important to pay attention at school and get a good education.
(d) Discuss word meanings, in particular, 'respiration'.
(e) After dictation, ask the pupils to design an invitation to a party and fill it in with the date of the party and an address where the party will be held.

Soft c

a c **c** e n t
a c **c** e s s
a c **c** e p t
a c **c** e l e r a t e
a c **c** i d e n t

c i r c l e
c i r c u s
c i r c u m f e r e n c e
c i r c u m s t a n c e s

n o t i **c** e
n o t i **ce** a b l y
o f f i **c** e
p r a c t i **c** e
p r o **c** e e d
p r o **c** e s s
r e **c** e i v e
s u c **c** e s s
s u c **c** e e d

c r i t i **c** i s m
d e **c** i d e
e x **c** i t e d
e x **c** i t e d l y
m e d i **c** i n e

Dictate the Sam Story

Sam is riding home on his bike. He is running late and decides to accelerate. He does not notice a huge hole in the road. The circumference of the hole is over a metre. Sam proceeds to crash into the hole and fall off his bike. His mobile phone smashes on the ground. He accepts help from a passer-by and calls Sue at work to tell her he has had an accident. Sue leaves her office and comes to get Sam. She picks up some medicine on her way, which Sam is happy to receive as his leg is starting to hurt. His trip has not been a success.

Teaching Points

(a) Remind that a 'c' is usually soft when followed by an 'e', 'i' or 'y'.
(b) Listen to both sounds (hard and soft) in the 'acc' and 'succ' words.
(c) Look at the underlined tricky parts – particularly draw attention to the 'e' in 'noticeably' (otherwise the 'a' would make the 'c' hard).
(d) Point out that 'cir' usually indicates something is round.
(e) Discuss the noun 'practice'. Talk about 'football practice' or 'band practice' – meaning rehearsal. Remember – it is not the verb.
(f) After dictation, ask the pupils to write a made-up interview with the passer-by who helped Sam where a description is given of the accident from the passer-by's point of view.

Double consonant/short vowel 2

a **gg** r e s s i v e
n e c e s s a r y
s u **cc** e s s
a **cc** o **mm** o d a t i o n
a **cc** o m p a n i m e n t
a **nn** o y
a **nn** o y e d
a **pp** a r a t u s

b r i **ll** i a n t
b i **tt** e r
c o **ll** e c t
c o **ll** e c t i o n
r e c o **ll** e c t
d i **ff** i c u l t
e x a **gg** e r a t e
p a **ss** a g e
p a **ss** e n g e r

r u **b b** i s h
s c r i **b b** l e
s u **m m** i t
t r a **f f** i c
t u **n n** e l

Dictate the Sam Story

A collection of rubbish stopped traffic using the Channel Tunnel on Tuesday. As Sam and Sue returned to England from summer holidays in France, they and other passengers became annoyed and aggressive when they were told it would be necessary to take the boat instead of the tunnel. Bitter arguments broke out, until a brilliant piece of apparatus, like a giant vacuum cleaner, entered the tunnel. Drivers and passengers cheered as it successfully sucked up the rubbish. Sam and Sue were glad to get home.

Teaching Points
(a) Remind about listening to long and short vowels – then deciding on one, or two, consonants.
(b) Talk about the tricky parts underlined – only one 'c' in necessary and the 'ar' in apparatus and necessary.
(c) Talk about other methods of crossing the English Channel – boat, hovercraft, plane, train and even swimming.
(d) Point out the word 'vacuum' and discuss its unusual spelling, and also, briefly, what a vacuum is.
(e) After dictation, ask the pupils to write a different story about a blocked tunnel in no more than 150 words.

ful

art**ful**	peac*e***ful**
bea<u>u</u>ti**ful**	ski<u>l</u>**ful**
delight**ful**	su<u>cc</u>e<u>ss</u>**ful**
fulfi<u>l</u>	thought**ful**
grat*e***ful**	truth**ful**
help**ful**	wast*e***ful**
hop*e***ful**	wi<u>l</u>**ful**
pain**ful**	wonder**ful**

Dictate the Sam Story

Sam and Sue have got a new puppy. They have named her Rose and they think she is delightful. She is also very wilful and pulls on her lead. She is skilful at getting Sam to give her lots of treats by making sweet faces at him. Sam likes to feed the puppy with chicken and Rose thinks it tastes wonderful but Sue thinks this is wasteful. They are hopeful that they will be successful in house-training her. Rose may make a mess of their house, but when she sleeps she looks so peaceful.

Teaching Points

(a) Remind pupils that when 'ful' is added to a word, either as a prefix, or as a suffix, only one 'l' is used.

(b) The same applies to other words, normally having double 'l', when used as a prefix or a suffix. Indicate 'fulfil', 'skilful', 'wilful'.

(c) Discuss unknown word meanings (artful, skilful, wilful).

(d) Because the only common spelling pattern is 'ful', discuss the other families that these words belong to:
   (i)   the silent 'e' in grateful, hopeful and wasteful.
   (ii) the 'igh' in delightful.
   (iii) the 'ea' in beautiful and peaceful.
   (iv) Link 'wonderful' with the 'm<u>o</u>ther and s<u>o</u>n' family.
   (v)   Remind about the pitfalls in 'su<u>cc</u>essful' and discuss why these consonants are doubled.
   Looking at the individual features of words aids memory.

ch (k)

Christmas	**ch**ord
Christ	**ch**or<u>al</u>
Christ<u>ian</u>	**ch**orus
christ<u>en</u>ing	(**ch**oir)
Christopher	or**ch**estra
Christine	
	a**ch**e
chaos	an**ch**or
chaotic	ar**ch**itect
character	e**ch**o
chemist	s**ch**eme
chromium	s**ch**ool
chr<u>y</u>salis	s**ch**olarship
chr<u>y</u>san<u>the</u>mum	stom<u>a</u>**ch**
	te**ch**nical

Dictate the Sam Story

Sam is the caretaker of St. Christopher's School, and each year there is a school summer concert. It is June, and the concert is only a week away. The music teachers are making preparations and there is choir and orchestra practice every afternoon. The sounds they make echo all over the school and Sam likes to sing along with the chorus. Sam decides to bring his new puppy, Rose, to the concert, but chaos breaks out when she jumps on the loudspeakers and causes a technical problem. Sam has a bad feeling in his stomach. He thinks he is going to get the sack, but Rose is so sweet he is let off the hook.

Teaching Points

(a) Point out that in this family, 'ch' is saying 'k'.
(b) The first group of words begin with 'Christ' and can be discussed in a manner appropriate to the pupils.
(c) The third group of words are all connected with music. Discuss what an orchestra is and what a choir is. Also discuss meanings of 'chord' and 'chorus'. Use pictures and recordings to give the pupils a sense of how big an orchestra or choir can be.
(d) Meanings of other words (architect, anchor, chemist) should be discussed.
(e) Point out that 'y' is saying 'i' in chrysalis and chrysanthemum and address any problems this may cause.
(f) Ask the pupils to write an article, in no more than 150 words, with the word 'chaos' in the title.

ly

equ<u>al</u>**l**y	definit<u>e</u>**l**y
fin<u>al</u>**l**y	excit<u>e</u>d**l**y
gradu<u>al</u>**l**y	immediat<u>e</u>**l**y
nat<u>ur</u>al**l**y	notic<u>e</u>ab**l**y
r<u>eal</u>**l**y	spars<u>e</u>**l**y
usual**l**y	
	fami**l**y
beautiful**l**y	particul<u>ar</u>**l**y
hopeful**l**y	probab**l**y
successful**l**y	quiet**l**y
truthful**l**y	tru**l**y
wonderful**l**y	volunt<u>a</u>ri**l**y
	w<u>h</u>ol**l**y

Dictate the Sam Story

Sam's friend Gus has gradually become part of Sam's family. When they met, Sam and Gus really liked each other immediately, and so naturally Sam's wife, Sue, liked him too. Gus is a tramp, so he is not used to people treating him kindly and equally, but as he has spent more time with Sam and Sue, he has become noticeably happier. Without them, Gus would probably have spent Christmas on his own, but now he definitely gets excited about waking up on Christmas morning and spending the day with his new family.

Teaching Points

(a) If 'ly' is added to a word which already ends in 'l', then the 'l' is doubled, as in the two groups in the first column.
(b) If a word is in the 'silent e' family as in the first group in the second column then the 'e' remains when 'ly' is added.
(c) Discuss word meanings not in the dictation (wholly, sparsely etc)
(d) Talk about Christmas, and other religious festivals from around the world, and find out which, if any, the pupils celebrate.
(e) Talk about the importance of being kind to people who are not just like ourselves.
(f) After dictation, ask the pupils to write a short description of their own family, in no more than 100 words.

or

absorb
assorted
carnivorous
decorate
evaporate
export
extraordinary

fortunate
history
humorous
important
northern

opportunity
organ
orchard
ordinary
ornament
performance
portrait
support
sword
vigorously

collector
equator
junior
senior
mayor
sponsor

Dictate the Sam Story

Sam, Sue and Gus are on the train to Yorkshire, in the northern part of England, to watch Sue's brother, Joe, give a performance on his organ. It is a very important concert for Joe and he is glad to have his family there for support. The mayor has also come along with assorted senior members of the local council. Joe is an extraordinary organ player, and when he plays, the music absorbs him. After the concert, the mayor presents Joe with a portrait of himself. Joe is pleased with the portrait as he is a keen art collector. He has had a great day.

Teaching Points
(a) Indicate in red where the 'or' digraph comes in each word.
(b) Pay special attention to the words where the speech sound is 'er'.
(c) Discuss what an organ is, showing pictures and playing recordings.
(d) Discuss other unknown meanings (e.g. carnivorous).
(e) Discuss the importance of art, and show a small selection of well-known works of art and ask how the pupils interpret them.
(f) After dictation, ask the pupils to get into pairs and draw a portrait of one another.

Silent Letters 1

w	**k**
w r a p	**k** n e e
w r e c k	**k** n e e l
w r e c k a g e	**k** n e l t
w r e **s** t l e r	**k** n i f e
w r e **s** t l i n g	**k** n i t
w r i t e	**k** n o b
w r i <u>t t</u> e n	**k** n o c k
w r o n g	**k** n o c k e r
a n s **w** e r	**k** n o t
s **w** o r d	**k** n o w
	k n e w

g	**c**
g n a t	s **c** e n e
g n a r l e d	s **c** e n e r y
g n a w	s **c** e n t
g n o m e	s **c** i e n c e
s i **g** n	s **c** i e n t i s t
	s **c** i <u>s s</u> o r <u>s</u>

Dictate the Sam Story

Sam and Sue think their garden is a bit of a wreck. When they look out of the window they would like to see some nice scenery, but they do not know how to go about it. Gus knows the answer. He hands them both a pair of scissors, and takes a knife for himself, and they start to cut back all the plants that are all gnarled and overgrown. Then Gus kneels down and places three happy looking gnomes in the middle of the garden. It is a lovely scene. The three of them have gnat bites on their arms and blisters on their knees, but all agree that the garden is much better.

Teaching Points
(a) Help the pupils to observe the silent letters and to talk about them. This will help them to remember and also to form good habits for the future.
(b) Point out that wrestle and wrestling have two silent letters.
(c) Discuss the other word family patterns within this group (double consonants in 'written' and 'scissors').
(d) Discuss word meanings (gnarled, gnaw, sign).
(e) Check that meanings of write, knot, know, knew, scene and scent are not confused with other words that sound the same. Put these words into appropriate sentences – neither use, not write the others at this stage.
(f) After dictation, ask the pupils to write a short description of their garden, or a favourite park, in no more than 100 words.

Silent Letters 2

```
           u                              n
     b u i l d                  a u t u m n
     b u i l d e r              c o n d e m n
   b i s c u i t                  c o l u m n
   d i s g u i s e                    h y m n
       g u e s s
       g u e s t
       g u i d e
       g u a r d
       g u i l t y
       g u a r a n t e e
   t o n g u e
     v a g u e

           t
     c a s t l e
     f a s t e n
 u n f a s t e n
     l i s t e n
     o f t e n
     t h i s t l e
     w h i s t l e
```

Dictate the Sam Story

The summer is nearly over and autumn is coming, so Sam decides to get some builders in to paint his house while the sun is still shining. Sam and Sue's new garden looks so smart, so they want their house to look just as good. The builders arrive and Sam makes them some tea and biscuits. They guarantee to have the job done by the end of the week, which Sue is happy about as they have guests coming for the weekend. The builders often whistle as they work, and Sam likes to lie in his garden with his gnomes and listen to them.

Teaching Points

(a) Again – discuss the silent letters and observe their positions within words.
(b) Discuss other family groups within this group (castle, fasten etc, where 'a' = 'ar').
(c) Talk about what a 'guarantee' is.
(d) Discuss other unknown word meanings in this group.
(e) Talk about the passing of the seasons and the characteristics of each.
(f) After dictation, ask the pupils to write a short story, of no more than 150 words, called 'The Forgotten Castle'.

ough/eigh

ough

th**ough**t
th**ough**tless
th**ough**tful
br**ough**t
ought
f**ough**t
n**ough**t

alth**ough**
th**ough**
d**ough**

dr**ough**t
b**ough**
pl**ough**

r**ough**
en**ough**
t**ough**
c**ough**
tr**ough**

thr**ough**
thr**ough**out

tho**rough**
tho**rough**ly
bo**rough**

eigh

eight
w**eigh**t
eighteen
n**eigh**b<u>our</u>
(for**eig**n)

Dictate the Sam Story

It has been a long hot summer and Sam is worried about his garden. No rain has fallen in England for the last eighteen weeks. There is not even enough water for washing and cleaning, although through careful controls, drinking supplies remain. Farmers cannot plough land because it is too dry and water troughs have to be filled by hand. Life is rough for the farmers throughout the country. Thoughtless people are wasting water by allowing taps to drip and there is a hosepipe ban, so Sam cannot water his plants. All his neighbours are in the same situation. In some foreign countries, it is even hotter and the drought is worse. Sam hopes the rain comes soon.

Teaching Points

(a) Talk about the 'look alike – sound different' aspects of 'ough'.
(b) Talk about the 'eigh' words, including 'foreign' even though it is slightly foreign to this word family!
(c) Draw attention to the ending of neighbour (English spelling only).
(d) Discuss any unknown word meanings.
(e) Discuss the importance of water, and the effects of drought around the world. Ask if any of the pupils have ever experienced a drought.
(f) After dictation, ask the pupils to write a letter or email of around 100 words to their local government representative on the subject of conserving water to avoid drought.

Soft g

a**ge**	**gi**ant
dam**age**	**gi**gantic
im**age**	**gi**psy
man**age**	ima**gi**ne
man**age**able	reli**gi**on
unman**age**able	
man**age**r	**Ge**orge
mess**age**	**Ge**orgina
messen**ge**r	**ge**ography
post**age**	**ge**neration
r**age**	**ge**nerosity
ramp**age**	hu**ge**
salv**age**	knowle<u>d</u>**ge**
	knowle<u>d</u>**ge**able
gym	privile**ge**
gymnasium	ser**ge**ant
gymnast	tra**ge**dy
ener**gy**	ve**ge**table

Dictate the Sam Story

Sam's niece Georgina is a brilliant gymnast. Sam and Sue sometimes go and watch her when she has a gymnastics competition. They are both amazed by her skill and energy and wonder how she manages to back flip off a huge box and spin through the air without doing herself any damage. Sam cannot imagine how anyone could be so brave, let alone a twelve-year-old girl! She is a different generation to him. Sam and Sue want to give Georgina a gift for her birthday and so they decide to pay for a new gymnastics kit. Georgina is very pleased, and thanks them for their generosity.

Teaching Points
(a) Discuss the various groups – 'age', 'ge', 'gi', and 'gy'. Remind that, usually if a 'g' is followed by an 'e', 'i', or 'y', it is soft.
(b) Look particularly at knowledgeable and sergeant in the list. Explain how the 'e' is essential to protect the 'g' from the 'a'.
(c) Point out silent 'd' in 'knowledge' and 'knowledgeable'.
(d) Discuss word meanings, in particular 'generation'. Pupils might bring in family photographs of three or four generations.
(e) Discuss what a gymnast is, and show pictures or video clips. Ask the pupils to discuss their own attempts at gymnastics.
(f) Discuss forms of energy – personal and power, and how we can maximise our energy.
(g) After dictation, ask the pupils to write a short report (around 100 words) on how they can keep their energy levels high and remain healthy.

ar

I	II
a r c t i c	<u>a</u> w k w **a r** d
a r g u m e n t	a f t e r w **a r** d s
a r t i s t	a p p **a** r a t u s
a r <u>ch</u> i t e c t	b a c k w **a r** d
b **a r** g <u>ai</u> n	b u r g l **a r**
c **a r** d i g a n	c o w **a r** d
c **a r** g <u>o</u>	c u s t **a r** d
c **a r** t <u>o</u> n	f o r w **a r** d
c o m p **a r** t m e n t	o r c h **a r** d
	p **a r** t i c u l **a r** l y
d e p **a r** t m e n t	
j **a r** g o n	p r e p **a** r a t i o n
m **a r** m <u>a</u> l a d e	r e g u l **a r**
m **a r** g **a** r i n e	s e p **a** r a t e
p **a r** l i <u>a</u> m e n t	s e p **a** r a t i o n
r e g **a r** d s	
r e m **a r** k a b l e	r e w **a r** d
s t **a** <u>r</u> t l e	t o w **a r** d s
s t **a** r v e	

Dictate the Sam Story

As a reward for all the charity work she does in schools, Sue has been invited to visit Parliament. Sam is going with her and they have been looking forward to the trip for weeks. On the day, they get up early, but Sue is too excited to eat her toast with margarine and marmalade, so Sam eats it for her. Sue has a new cardigan to wear so she looks very smart. When they arrive, Sue and Sam look round the education department, and afterwards they go for lunch. Sue is glad as she thought she might starve after missing breakfast. She has big bowl of apple pie and custard for her pudding.

Teaching Points
(a) Discuss the difference in sound between the words in group I and those in group II. In group II 'ar' looks the same, but sounds 'er'.
(b) Discuss other word families within this family ('ch' in architect, 't' in startle, 'aw' in awkward).
(c) Point out the tricky parts of bargain and parliament and that 'ar' appears twice in 'particularly' and sounds different each time.
(d) 'Reward' and 'towards' look the same – and again sound different.
(e) Discuss Parliament – what it is for, how it works and its history.
(f) Discuss the main political parties in your country, their leaders and why it is important to vote in an election when you are old enough.
(g) After dictation, ask the pupils to write a short history of their Parliament, in no more than 150 words.

ous

fam**ous**	**cious**
humor**ous**	atro**cious**
jeal**ous**	cons**cious**
marvell**ous**	uncons**cious**
nerv**ous**	pre**cious**
ridicul**ous**	spa**cious**
carniv<u>or</u>**ous**	suspi**cious**
conif<u>er</u>**ous**	
por**ous**	an<u>x</u>**ious**
vigor**ous**	con<u>scie</u>n<u>t</u>**ious**

ious

cur**ious**
env**ious**
industr**ious**
myster**ious**
prev**ious**
ser**ious**

Dictate the Sam Story

Sam is anxious about a curious animal that has made its home amongst the coniferous trees at the bottom of his garden. The animal seems to be carnivorous, as bones of chicken, turkey and rabbit have been found amongst the fir cones beneath the trees. Sam is nervous about the animal, but Sue finds the whole matter quite humorous and will not take it seriously. Sue thinks it is ridiculous that Sam is so concerned, but Sam is very conscientious. He wants to call a famous animal expert called Dr. Silver, to get his thoughts on the animal. Sue thinks the garden is quite spacious and the animal should be left alone.

Teaching Points
(a) Discuss each group in turn. The common factor is 'ous'. Point out that 'ci' is saying 'sh' and that this sound can also be heard in 'anxious' and 'conscientious'.
(b) Talk about carnivorous animals, using pictures.
(c) Discuss other unknown words on the list.
(d) Discuss coniferous trees with cones, twigs and pictures, and how they are different from deciduous trees.
(e) Talk about abbreviations of titles – Dr, Mr, Mrs, Miss etc.
(f) After dictation, ask the pupils to each draw their idea of the 'Mysterious Animal' and describe it underneath in no more than 50 words.

ary/able

nece<u>ss</u>**ary**	**able**
volunt**ary**	veg<u>e</u>t**able**
li<u>br</u>**ary**	mis<u>er</u>**able**
contemp<u>o</u>r**ary**	av<u>ai</u>l**able**
temp<u>o</u>r**ary**	disagr<u>ee</u>**able**
suppl<u>e</u>ment**ary**	comp<u>a</u>r**able**
compl<u>i</u>ment**ary**	manag<u>e</u>**able**
station**ary**	knowledg<u>e</u>**able**
ordin**ary**	reason**able**
extraordin**ary**	
Fe<u>br</u>u**ary**	
Janu**ary**	
Hung**ary**	

Dictate the Sam Story

Sue is pleased because a new library is to be built in the centre of town. In January the old library will close and it will be necessary to move all the books into a temporary building. As this will take time it will be February before books are available for borrowing again. Sam and Sue are helping to move the books on a voluntary basis. There are thousands of books to move, but with help from local people, the task is manageable. The new library is an exciting, contemporary building and when it is ready, Sue thinks it will be extraordinary.

Teaching Points

(a) Discuss both endings. Over-emphasise the 'a' sound so that pupils listen and relate to it.
(b) Point out the underlined tricky parts:
   (i) 'or' in contemporary and temporary.
   (ii) 'r' in library and February.
   (iii) the difference in sound, and therefore letter, in supplementary and complimentary.
   (iv) the 'ge' in vegetable, manageable and knowledgeable.
   (v) 'er' in miserable and 'ai' in available.
(c) Discuss word meanings – stationary, contemporary, and temporary.
(d) Discuss other unknown words.
(e) After dictation, ask the pupils to write 100 words on why libraries are important.

le

ang**le**	responsib**le**
Bib**le**	samp**le**
examp**le**	scramb**le**
ho<u>rr</u>ib**le**	scribb**le**
id**le**	sensib**le**
visib**le**	simp**le**
invisib**le**	
	sing**le**
jung**le**	trif**le**
mirac**le**	unc**le**
pebb**le**	
possib**le**	
impossib**le**	
princip**le**	
probab**le**	

Dictate the Sam Story

Gus has always had a dream to visit the jungle, but it has not been possible because he has never been able to afford it. But then, by some miracle, a rich uncle he never knew had died and left Gus all his money. In the past, Gus has been idle and not very responsible, but now a trip to the jungle is probable, so he has a burst of energy. Sam is not sure if it is sensible for Gus to go alone, and uses the example of a single man in the news who went last year and never came back. Gus will not change his mind though, and he books his plane ticket. They celebrate by eating a huge trifle.

Teaching Points

(a) 'le' is the most common way of making the 'l' sound at the end of words.
(b) Draw attention to the in/im prefixes.
(c) Discuss 'principle' in terms of rules, laws, honesty etc. Think of good role models, or 'people of principle', so that this spelling of the word is underlined in the pupils' minds.
(d) Before dictation, discuss the idea of miracles.
(e) Discuss jungles and rainforests around the world. Using pictures, talk about why these areas are important, including the wildlife that can be found there.
(f) After dictation, ask the pupils to write a short story called, 'My Miracle' in no more than 150 words. It can be about anything that has happened to them that they consider special or unusual.

er

adv**er**tis**e**ment	p**er**s**u**ade
beak**er**	ref**err**ed
charact**er**	temp**er**_a_ture
circumf**er**ence	th**er**mom**e**t**er**
dag**g**er	whisp**er**
desp**er**ate	monast**er**y
draw**er**	jewell**er**
exa**gg**erate	jewell**er**y
fi**er**y	station**er**
int**err**upt	station**er**y
Medit**err**anean	
murd**er**	
murd**er**er	
o**ff**er	
res**er**v_oi_r	
res**er**v_oi_rs	

Dictate the Sam Story

Sam has seen an advertisement for a cheap holiday at a resort beside the Mediterranean Sea. The offer includes flights and a hotel. He wants to persuade Sue to take time off work and go away. He can see from the thermometer he has on the side of his house that the temperature in England is very low, and he thinks they could do with a bit of sunshine. He asks Sue what she thinks, but she says she has seen in the news that there was a murder at the hotel in the advertisement, and a dagger was found in one of the rooms. This is why the holiday is so cheap! They decide to stay at home and hope it gets sunny.

Teaching Points
(a) Discuss the tricky parts, in particular the words with double 'r' – where one belongs to the 'er' sound and the next is the first consonant of the new syllable.
(b) Look at the three syllables in mur/der/er, the 'u' in persuade and the 'a' in temperature.
(c) Discuss reservoirs and their uses. Point out that this actually a French word, which is why it has an unusual ending.
(d) With the use of maps, talk about the Mediterranean Sea and countries around it. If any pupils have been on holiday there, ask them to describe their trip.
(e) Discuss what a monastery is, and also monks, nuns and convents.
(f) After dictation, ask the pupils to write a short description of their favourite holiday in no more than 150 words.

y (ĭ)

mystery	sympathy
mysterious	sympathetic
crystal	system
crypt	systematic
cymbals	syllable
Egypt	symptom
gym	syrup
gymnasium	syringe
gymnast	

hymn
lyrics
physics
physical education (P.E.)
pyjamas
pyramid
rhythm
sycamore

Dictate the Sam Story

It is after lunch and Sam is still in bed in his pyjamas. He is feeling ill and Sue is very sympathetic. Sam's symptoms are a bad cough and a sore throat. Sue has given him some cough syrup, but he is not getting any better so she calls the doctor. Dr. Jones comes to see Sam. He injects some strong medicine into Sam's arm with a syringe and takes his temperature. Dr. Jones tells Sam to stay in bed for the rest of the week. He also thinks Sam is a bit unfit, and this is partly what is making him ill. He tells Sam and Sue they must do more physical activity, and maybe even join a gym. Sam groans – he hated physical education at school.

Teaching Points

(a) Link gym, gymnasium, gymnast and physical education. Discuss the shortening of gymnasium to gym, and physical education to P.E.
(b) Discuss the word 'symptoms' – what it means, and how recognising symptoms can help us get the medical attention we need.
(c) Discuss the musical words in this family – hymn, rhythm, cymbals, symphony, and also lyrics. Use pictures and recordings to illustrate the differences.
(d) Discuss what it feels like to be a doctor or a nurse. See if any of the pupils would like to become either of these, and what sort of qualifications they would need.
(e) Discuss how keeping fit keeps us healthy, and why P.E. is important.
(f) Talk about Egypt, showing it on the map and explaining some of the history.
(g) After dictation, ask the pupils to write a short story called 'The Mystery of the Pyramids in Egypt'. It should be no more than 200 words.

sion

admi**ssion**
discu**ssion**
mi**ssion**
permi**ssion**
posse**ssion**
proce**ssion**
profe**ssion**

confu**sion**
deci**sion**
divi**sion**
ero**sion**
excur**sion**
explo**sion**
inva**sion**

occa**sion**
provi**sion**
vi**sion**
televi**sion**

Dictate the Sam Story

Sam and Gus are watching the news on television. There are two scientists having a discussion about a space mission to Mars, which the European Space Agency is planning. Even though it will be a risky mission, with a high chance of explosions on the space shuttle, they have made the decision to go ahead. There is some division amongst the scientists about whether enough provision has been made to save the shuttle if there is an explosion. Sam has an admission to make to Gus – anything about science leaves him in a state of total confusion. Gus is worried there may be an alien invasion after the mission.

Teaching Points

(a) Remind pupils that the 'tion' family was discussed several weeks earlier and mention that 'tion' is the larger family.
(b) Look at the words in group 1 – 'ssion'. Learn these. There are very few other common words in this group.
(c) The sound of the next group is slightly different and this will be the indication of the ending. Listen and discuss the sounds.
(d) Discuss the meanings of unknown words.
(e) Talk about space travel and why it might be important.
(f) Discuss spellings of science and scientist, preferably before dictation.
(g) After dictation, ask the pupils to write a short piece called 'Rocket Launch'. No more than 100 words.

ie/ei

n**ie**ce	f**ie**ld
br**ie**f	sh**ie**ld
bel**ie**f	y**ie**ld
bel**ie**ve	
ch**ie**f	f**ie**rce
handkerch**ie**f	p**ie**rce
gr**ie**f	p**ie**rcing
gr**ie**ve	
	re**ce**ive
misch**ie**f	**ce**iling
ach**ie**ve	con**ce**it
s**ie**ge	con**ce**ited
bes**ie**ge	de**ce**it
p**ie**ce	de**ce**itful
mantelp**ie**ce	de**ce**ive
pr**ie**st	but
shr**ie**k	s**ei**ze

Dictate the Sam Story

Sam has niece called Mary. She is full of fun and mischief, and often plays tricks on Sam. Today she is trying to deceive him into thinking that a plate of mud is a piece of chocolate cake. Sam does not believe Mary, as he knows she can be deceitful. He decides to play a trick on her. He picks up the mud in his handkerchief and hides it on the mantelpiece. He puts a real piece of cake on the plate and eats it. Mary lets out a piercing shriek, as she thinks that Sam is eating mud. Sam laughs, and then so does Mary when he shows her what he has done.

Teaching Points

(a) Learn and link with this group – 'i before e except after c'.
(b) Draw attention to the 'ie' words in the first four groups – and then to the 'ei' words in group five.
(c) Draw attention to the f/ve words. (Belief and grief are nouns – believe and grieve are verbs). Put words into sentences to illustrate meanings and parts of speech.
(d) Draw attention to 'field' family and 'fierce' family.
(e) Discuss any unknown words, such as siege and besiege, and give contexts for these words.
(f) Look at 'seize' and discuss this exception.
(g) After dictation, ask the children to write a short story called 'The Piercing Shriek' in no more than 150 words.

ent/ence

argum**ent**	parliam**ent**
accompanim**ent**	persist**ent**
announcem**ent**	promin**ent**
appar**ent**	suffi**ci**ent
comp*li*m**ent**	
developm**ent**	differ**ence**
differ**ent**	comm**ence**
excitem**ent**	conveni**ence**
	sent**ence**
experim**ent**	ref*er***ence**
effi**ci**ent	cons**ci**ence
magnific**ent**	experi**ence**
inconveni**ent**	obed*i***ence**
ingredi**ent**s	intelli*g***ence**
independ**ent**	
innoc**ent**	
intellig**ent**	
obedi**ent**	

Dictate the Sam Story

Gus has an announcement to make to Sam and Sue. He can barely contain his excitement. After years of being a tramp, he has decided to try something different. He wants to become a cook and start an independent café. He has lots of experience, he makes magnificent food for his friends, and he is very intelligent. Sam and Sue think it is a great idea. Gus needs them to give him a reference so he can get a loan from the bank to buy ingredients. Then his new job can commence. Sam hopes Gus has the persistence to make his café a success.

Teaching Points
(a) Encourage pupils not only to look at the ending of these words, but also the syllables, particularly with words like 'accompaniment', 'magnificent', 'ingredients'. Suggest that they say the syllables as they write them, then ensure that they leave none out.
(b) Draw attention to the 'ci' words.
(c) Point out the two distinct groups 'ent' and 'ence' and how linked words change according to context e.g. different becomes difference.
(d) Discuss the word 'café' and its French origin.
(e) Discuss unknown word meanings such as apparent, prominent, reference.
(f) Talk about the qualities a person may need to set up an independent business, and about the pros and cons of working for yourself.
(g) After dictation, ask the pupils to think of their favourite food, and then write the recipe, with a list of ingredients.

al ending

arriv**al**
annu**al**
carniv**al**
cathedr**al**
centr**al**
<u>ch</u>or**al**
crimin**al**
cymb**al**

equ**al**
festiv**al**
fin**al**
fat**al**
loc**al**
mamm**al**
materi**al**
music**al**

natur**al**
na<u>tion</u>**al**
profe<u>ssion</u>**al**
punctu**al**
unpunctu**al**
princip**al**
origin**al**
remov**al**

usu**al**
usu**al**ly
so<u>ci</u>**al**
spe<u>ci</u>**al**
espe<u>ci</u>**al**ly

Dictate the Sam Story

Sue has a good singing voice, and she is one of the principal singers in her local choir. She is on her way to perform in the annual music festival at the cathedral, but her train is running late. Sue is usually very punctual and is anxious that her late arrival will mean she will miss her solo. Luckily, the rail delays are on a national scale, and so lots of members of the choral group are also running late. They are all in such a rush when they do finally get to the cathedral that they do not have time to change into smart clothes. But they are so professional, they still give a very musical performance.

Teaching Points
(a) Look at the other families (tion, sion, ch (k), ci and double consonants) within this family.
(b) Discuss annual events – school, local, national.
(c) Discuss festivals and carnivals, such as the Notting Hill Carnival and carnival season in Brazil. Show pictures of the costumes involved and play excerpts of the kind of music used.
(d) Talk about choral music, again with use of recordings. Compare choral music with carnival music.
(e) Talk about principal, as distinct from principle, meaning chief, head or most important.
(f) After dictation, ask the pupils to write an article called 'Late Arrival'. No more than 150 words.

y (i)

cycle	nylon
bicycle	occupy
tricycle	plywood
ally	three-ply
apply	pry
a<u>w</u>ry	python
deny	rhyme
defy	reply
hyacinth	style
hydrofoil	stylist
lying	tyrant
multiply	

Dictate the Sam Story

Sam is riding his bicycle down a narrow path when he sees what looks like a python lying in the road. He stops cycling, and gets off to take a closer look. He calls Gus on his phone, but he does not reply so Sam has to work out what to do on his own. He sees that the python has got its head stuck under a stone. He grabs a piece of plywood from a skip, and tries to pry the stone up and away so the python can move. He hopes his plan does not go awry – he has heard that snakes can multiply if they are cut in half. The stone rolls to the side, and the python slides into the bushes.

Teaching Points

(a) Listen to the sound 'y' is making in these words. Link with easier words – my, cry, try etc.
(b) Talk about 'bi' and 'tri' when prefixes of cycle.
(c) Look at the silent letters in awry and rhyme.
(d) Discuss unknown words such as hydrofoil, nylon, plywood etc, using pictures where necessary.
(e) Show pictures of pythons, and ask if anyone has seen one up close, or perhaps even keeps one as a pet.
(f) After dictation, pupils should write the next instalment choosing their own title. No more than 150 words.

ea (ē)

b**ea**ker	**ea**v**e̲s**drop	str**ea**k
b**ea**t	**ea**s**i̲**ly	tr**ea**c**l̲e**
unb**ea**t**e̲**n	gr**ea**se	tr**ea**t
b**ea**u̲tiful	gr**ea**sy	p**ea**ce
c**ea**se	id**ea**l	w**ea**ve
cr**ea**tu̲r̲e̲	l**ea**gu̲e	w̲h̲**ea**t
dis**ea**se	s**ea**l	r**ea**lly
eagl̲e̲		

ear

h**ear**	t**ear**s
f**ear**	w**ear**y
f**ear**less	w**ear**ily
n**ear**ly	y**ear**
sh**ear**s	y**ear**ly
sp**ear**	

Dictate the Sam Story

Gus has been working in his café for nearly a month now, and it is going really well. He has painted the front in beautiful colours, with streaks of red, yellow and green paint all over the door. He is planning a new treat for anyone who comes in to eat there. He has invented a way of making treacle-tart ice-cream. He melts the treacle in a pan, and then cracks eggs into a beaker. He beats the eggs into the treacle, adds cream and then puts it into the freezer to set. As soon as people hear about it, the café will be full.

Teaching Points
(a) Draw attention to the tricky parts underlined.
   (i) 'e' in unbeaten
   (ii) 'u' in beautiful and league
   (iii) 'e' in eavesdrop
   (iv) 'wh' in wheat
(b) Remind of the 'le' family. Eagle and treacle are in it.
(c) Remind of the 'ure' family and link creature with it.
(d) Look at 'easily' and 'wearily' and discuss how they have grown from 'easy' and 'weary'. (Changed the 'y' to 'i' and added 'ly').
(e) Look at 'ear' family words and draw attention to the common 'ear' unit.
(f) Discuss unknown words such as eavesdrop, ideal, weary, seal etc.
(g) After dictation, ask the pupils to write a short piece called 'Holiday Treat'. No more than 150 words.

our

armour
behaviour
colour
favour
favourite
flavour
harbour

courage
encourage
encouragement
discourage
flourish
nourish
tambourine

honour
honour<u>able</u>
dishonour<u>able</u>
humour
labour
neighbour
neighbourhood
rumour
vapour

Dictate the Sam Story

There is a horrible rumour going around Sam's neighbourhood that one of Sam's neighbours has been accused of dishonourable behaviour. It seems that the neighbour, who is a builder, was paid to carry out some labour on an old woman's house. The builder was supposed to paint the woman's house white, but he painted it the wrong colour. When the woman complained, the builder said he would not help. Sam thinks it took a lot of courage for the old woman to complain to the builder, and he is angry at the builder's behaviour. As a favour, Sam paints the old woman's house the right colour. He also makes a poster to discourage others from using that builder again.

Teaching Points

(a) Talk about 'our' saying 'er' at the end of these words.
(b) The group of words starting with 'courage' look the same and sound different. Listen to the different sounds in each group of words.
(c) Draw attention to the underlined letters.
(d) Discuss any unknown words, such as armour and harbour, using pictures where necessary.
(e) Relate honour to honest, and talk about honourable and dishonourable characters in stories and real life.
(f) Talk about prefixes 'en' and 'dis', particularly in relation to dishonourable and discourage.
(g) Discuss rumours, and when they can be unhelpful or even damaging.
(h) After dictation, ask the pupils to write a report called 'A Wild Rumour'. No more than 150 words.

ance/ant

balance
entrance
n**ui**sance
distance

attendance
performance
a**c**quaintance

appearance
all**i**ance
assistance
extravagance
ignorance
ins**u**rance

circumstances
substance

distant
elephant
ele**g**ant
extravagant
ignorant
s**er**g**e**ant
vacant

Dictate the Sam Story

Sue has always had a dream to see an elephant in the wild. She knows she and Sam would have to travel a long distance to make her dream come true. It would also be expensive, and Sue does not really approve of such extravagance. But Sam has a friend who is a sergeant in the army and travels a lot. The sergeant has spent some time in Africa, and knows of a vacant holiday home where they could stay quite cheaply. They will need to pay for flights and holiday insurance, but Sam thinks they can afford it. They make the trip and on day one, a huge elephant makes an appearance. The look on Sue's face makes it all worth it.

Teaching Points

(a) Draw attention to the underlined tricky parts.
(b) Look at the families within this family:
  (i) 'ear' in appearance
  (ii) 'ai' in acquaintance
  (iii) 'cir' in circumstances
  (iv) 'er' and 'or' in performance
  (v) 'or' in ignorance.
(c) Discuss the meanings of extravagant/extravagance. Let the pupils talk about the most extravagant thing they would like to do.
(d) Talk about insurance – against fire and burglary, car insurance and holiday insurance.
(e) Talk about safari holidays, and see if any of the pupils have been on one. Discuss how large animals such as elephants need a lot of space to be happy.
(f) After dictation, ask the pupils to look up 'elephant' and write a description of around 100 words.

Apostrophes

Dictate the Sam Story

It has been a wonderful year for Sam and Sue. They have sorted out their garden and painted all the garden gnomes' hats bright red. They have been to see concerts and Sue's singing has been praised all over town. Gus's café has been a great success, and now has got its own little garden, too. Sam's bike finally fell apart but it's very old. He got a new one. They also went on an amazing holiday, and saw elephants and lions. They watched three lionesses' cubs playing together. They brought home a shark's tooth as a gift for Gus. It's a good job they can now have a rest before Christmas.

Teaching Points

(a) Remind:
   (i) 'it's' is short for 'it is'.
   (ii) 'its' is the possessive.
   (iii) gnomes' and lionesses' – apostrophe after the 's', because it is plural.
(b) After dictation, discuss various combinations of 'it's' and 'its' and ask the pupils to come with three sentences of their own, which display use of shortened 'it is', singular possessive and plural possessive.
(c) Discuss reasons why people need to write, in school and as adults, and how it can help with work and also be a hobby too.